Learn to DRAW

Drawing
Knights
and
Castles

Jorge Santillan and Sarah Eason

Gareth Stevens
Publishing

Please visit our website, www.garethstevens.com. For a free color catalog of all our high-quality books, call toll free 1-800-542-2595 or fax 1-877-542-2596.

Library of Congress Cataloging-in-Publication Data

Eason, Sarah.
 Drawing knights and castles / Sarah Eason.
     pages cm. — (Learn to draw)
ISBN 978-1-4339-9541-5 (pbk.)
ISBN 978-1-4339-9542-2 (6-pack)
ISBN 978-1-4339-9540-8 (library binding)
1. Knights and knighthood in art—Juvenile literature. 2. Castles in art—Juvenile literature.
3. Drawing—Technique—Juvenile literature. I. Title.
 NC825.K54E27 2013
 743'.87—dc23

                          2012048247

Published in 2014 by
Gareth Stevens Publishing
111 East 14th Street, Suite 349
New York, NY 10003

© 2014 Gareth Stevens Publishing

Produced for Gareth Stevens by Calcium Creative Ltd
Illustrated by Jorge Santillan
Designed by Paul Myerscough
Edited by Rachel Blount

Printed in the United States of America

CPSIA compliance information: Batch CS13GS: For further information contact Gareth Stevens, New York, New York at 1-800-542-2595.

Contents

Learn to Draw!

Knights were great fighters from a long-ago time called the Middle Ages. Knights often fought on horseback, and were armed with huge swords, daggers, and heavy battle-axes. Life as a knight was dangerous and tough, and it took many years of training before a boy could finally call himself a knight. Find out more about knights and their castles, then learn how to draw them, too.

You will need:

Just a few simple pieces of equipment are needed to create wonderful drawings of knights:

Sketchpad or paper
Visit an art store to buy good quality paper.

Pencils
You will need both fine-tipped and thick-tipped pencils.

Eraser
Don't worry if you make a mistake—use an eraser to remove any unwanted lines. You can even use it to add highlights.

Paintbrush, paints, and pens
Buy a set of quality paints, brushes, and coloring pens to add color to your awesome drawings.

Into Battle

Knights were trained to fight in deadly battles. A knight was protected by his suit of armor. This was a covering of metal pieces joined together to make a suit that covered the body, legs, feet, arms, and hands of a knight. Knights also wore a metal helmet to protect their heads.

Step 1

Draw the knight's body, arms, hands, legs, and feet. Then draw his head and sword.

Step 2

Go over the lines you drew in step 1 to give your knight a softer outline. Add his shoulder plates, scabbard, and the helmet. Erase any unwanted lines.

Step 3

Add detail by drawing the visor, fingers, and the protective armor on the knight's knees and elbows.

Step 4

Draw the lines on the armor and add detail to the knight's visor and scabbard. Draw the spike on the knight's heel, too.

Step 5

Now begin to bring your picture to life by adding shading. Shade the slit in the knight's visor more deeply than the rest of the suit of armor.

Step 6

Now you can start to color your knight. Use a gray to color the suit of armor. Color the scabbard with a brilliant blue. Use gold for the tip of the scabbard and brown for the band across it. Use gold for the guard of the sword. Color the belt and the slit of the visor dark brown.

Step 7

Add light touches to the helmet, body armor, and the knight's sword for highlights. Your powerful knight is ready to fight any foe that comes near!

Armed to Fight

A knight's weapons included a large, wide, and heavy sword called a broadsword. The sword was so heavy that it had to be held and lifted with both hands. Knights also fought with a lighter sword and a dagger. A knight carried a shield into battle to protect himself.

A Knight's Castle

Knights were often the sons of noblemen. These were men who owned land and had servants who worked for them. A knight and his servants lived in a castle. Castles were large buildings made of stone. Many people lived and worked inside the castle walls.

Step 1

Draw the base of the castle, then add the columns of the turrets. Use a triangle shape for the tip of each turret.

Step 2

Add the shape of the foreground. Then draw the turrets' balconies, and the castle's doors, and the arches at the front of the castle. Add the two small turrets to the top right and top left.

Step 3

Now begin to add detail. Draw each turret window, then add the bricked edges of the balconies, arches, and the wall above the doors. Add a path leading to the castle.

Step 4

Draw bricks on the turrets and walls. Add more detail to the balconies, doors, and the path. Draw flags on the turrets.

Step 5

Now shade your castle's turrets, walls, and the doors. Add shading to the foreground, flags, and the castle pathway.

Step 6

Color your castle walls in a light lilac. Use blue for the tips of the turrets and a deep shade of purple-gray for the arches. Use dark gray for the turret windows and the windows below the arches. Color the doors brown and the flags bright red. The foreground should be brown with a white pathway.

Step 7

Add highlights to the castle walls, turrets, and the tips of the turrets. Use highlights for the flags and the castle foreground, too. Your fabulous castle is now complete and fit for any worthy knight!

Giant Towers

Castles had very tall towers called turrets. Windows were cut into the turrets so that people within the castle could see for many miles around. This helped them to see if enemy armies were about to attack the castle.

Into the Joust

Knights practiced their fighting at special tournaments called jousts. During the tournaments, knights showed off their skills by jousting. This was a competition in which two knights charged toward each other on horseback, holding a long pole called a lance. The knight that managed to knock the other off his horse won the joust.

Step 1

Draw the body, legs, neck, head, and tail of the horse. Then draw the body, legs, feet, arms, and head of your knight. Add the shield and lance.

Step 2

Go over the lines from step 1 to create a more rounded outline. Erase any unwanted lines. Then mark the features of the horse's face, its ears, and its mane. Draw the plume on the knight's helmet.

Step 3

Add detail by drawing the reins, saddle, bridle, and the horse's coat. Draw the outline of its eye. Add detail to the knight's armor, helmet, and the plume at its top.

Step 4

Draw the lines on the lance and visor. Then add detail to the horse's face, hooves, and saddle.

Step 5

Shade the horse's body, coat, and reins. Add shading to the lance and the knight's helmet, armor, and shield.

Step 6

Color the horse in a medium brown shade. Use a rich brown for the mane, eye, and tail. Use dark brown for the saddle, hooves, and the belt of the knight. Color the armor lilac, the shield red, and the reins, plume, and horse's coat blue. Color the lance white and red. Add the gold buckles.

Step 7

Add highlights to the horse, lance, shield, armor, and helmet of the knight to complete the picture. Your knight and horse are ready to face the joust!

Fighting on Foot

Knights also showed that they could fight on foot with swords and other battle weapons at jousts. People watched the fights in specially built stands, a little like the way we watch football or baseball games today.

Great Castles

During the time of knights, a lot of great castles were built. It took many years and many workers to build a castle. Huge stones were cut and then placed on top of each other to build the walls. A large, long pit was cut into the earth around the castle and filled with water. It was called a moat and was built to help keep enemies away from the castle walls.

Step 1

Draw the base of the castle, then add the building's tall, rectangular turret walls.

Step 2

Draw the tops of the turrets, then mark the drawbridge and the castle's windows.

Step 3

Add the bricked edges of the turret tips and the castle walls. Draw the lowering drawbridge and the water of the moat.

Step 4

Add the castle's flag and draw some bricks on its walls. Add detail to the drawbridge and shade the windows.

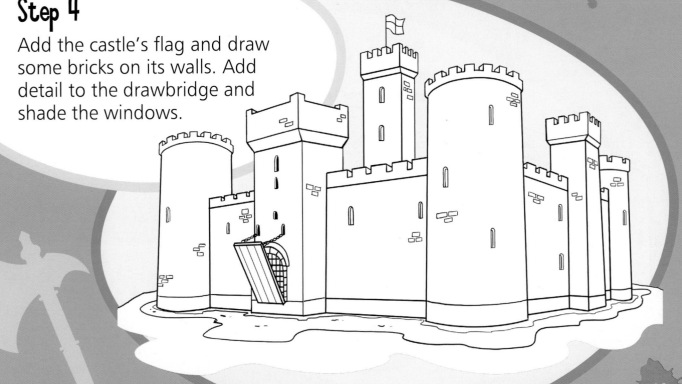

Step 5

Add further shading to the castle walls and turrets. Shade the drawbridge and moat.

Step 6

Now color the castle in a light beige color. Use a dark brown for the turret windows and drawbridge. Color the water blue and the flag yellow and red.

Step 7

Add highlights to the castle walls and moat. Use a brown shade to add detail to the bricks. Use a darker shade of blue to add depth to the water of the moat to complete the castle.

Stay Out!

A drawbridge was a huge front door that could be lifted or lowered with a chain or a rope. The people in the castle kept the drawbridge shut most of the time to help stop enemies from entering the castle.

A Coat of Arms

Knights showed who they were and which family they came from with a coat of arms. This was a picture or a pattern the knight used to decorate his shield. Favorite images used for a coat of arms were swans, dragons, and lions. The coat of arms was used in battle to show other fighters that the person they were fighting was a knight and not just an ordinary soldier.

Step 1

Draw your knight in a standing pose, battle-ax held aloft. Draw his body, legs, feet, arms, and hands. Then add his head, ax, and shield.

Step 2

Go over the lines from step 1 to create a softer outline. Mark the sections of the armor and helmet, and the coat of arms pattern on the shield.

22

Step 3

Draw the shape of the coat of arms, the visor, and add detail to the body armor, too.

Step 4

Draw the lines on the body armor and visor. Draw the edge of the shield and the spikes on the elbow, knee, and foot armor. Add detail to the head of the ax.

Step 5

Shade your knight's helmet, shield, armor, and battle-ax. Use deeper shading for the visor slit.

Step 6

Color the armor in a light yellow and a medium shade of olive green. Use lilac for the ax head and color the handle dark brown. Use light blue for the shield edge, a dark blue for the middle, and yellow for the center. Color the lion of the coat of arms light orange.

Step 7

Finally, add highlights to your knight's armor, battle-ax, and shield. Prepare for battle!

Living by the Rules

Knights had to live by a special set of rules called the code of chivalry. The rules included:
- Being honest and telling the truth.
- Helping people in need.
- Being brave.
- Always helping your king.
- Never showing off!

Wicked Knights

Some knights broke the code of chivalry and did not live by its rules. They often tried to steal other knights' castles so they could keep them for themselves. One of the most wicked of all knights was Mordred, an evil knight who killed King Arthur.

Step 1

Draw these two knights in a fighting pose. Draw the bodies, legs, feet, arms, and hands. Then add the heads, swords, and shields.

Step 2

Give your knights a softer outline and erase any unwanted lines. Add the helmet plumes, visors, and the shapes of the tunic and cloak.

Step 3

Add detail to the plumes, armor, coats of arms, swords, and visors. Give the knight on the left a cloak, too, and draw his face.

Step 4

Add further detail to the visors and armor of your knights.

27

Step 5

Shade your knights' armor, helmets, shields, swords, and cloaks. Don't forget to add shading to the visors and plumes.

Step 6

Color the armor of the left knight gray. Give him a blue cloak and a green plume. Add a green leaf to his shield. Color the armor of the right knight gray and purple. Color his cloak and plume red. Color his shield dark gray with a yellow sword.

Add light touches to the knights' armor, cloaks, weapons, shields, and plumes. Which knight do *you* think will win this fight?

King Arthur

Some of the most famous knight stories ever told are those of King Arthur and his Knights of the Round Table. Arthur is believed to be a great knight and famous ruler who may have lived in Great Britain around 1,500 years ago. Stories about Arthur were told by people for hundreds of years until they were written down in a book in the Middle Ages.

Glossary

armed to be carrying weapons such as swords and daggers

battle-ax a heavy ax used to fight

charged ran very quickly toward someone or something

dagger a short, sharp weapon a little like a sword

detail the fine lines on a drawing

enemies people who are against you

entering going inside

erase to remove

evil bad

foe an enemy

highlights the light parts on a picture

honest truthful, not lying

horseback riding on a horse

lance a long pole used to knock another knight off horseback during a joust

pit a hole

plume a bunch of feathers

pose the position a person or creature is in

protect to keep safe from harm

ruler someone who is in charge of other people

scabbard the protective covering of a sword. Knights kept their swords in scabbards when they were not using them to fight.

servants people who work for other people

shield a large piece of metal that was carried by knights to protect them against weapons when fighting in battle

skills useful things that someone can do

stands wooden benches on which people can sit, or areas in which they can stand to watch a show or competition

tournaments competitions

trained taught

turrets very tall stone towers on a castle

visor the movable part of a knight's helmet. Visors were at the front of the helmet and protected the knight's face.

wicked bad

For More Information

Books

Bergin, Mark. *How to Draw Knights and Castles*. New York, NY: PowerKids Press, 2012.

Levin, Freddy. *1-2-3 Draw Knights, Castles, and Dragons*. Mankato, MN: Peel Press, 2001.

Nishida, Masaki. *Drawing Manga Medieval Castles and Knights: How to Draw Manga*. New York, NY: PowerKids Press, 2007.

Websites

Find out more about knights and castles at:
webtech.kennesaw.edu/jcheek3/castles.htm

Discover more about the world of knights at:
www.kidspast.com/world-history/0208-lords-knights.php

Find even more knights and castles to draw at:
www.activityvillage.co.uk/knights_theme.htm

Publisher's note to educators and parents: Our editors have carefully reviewed these websites to ensure that they are suitable for students. Many websites change frequently, however, and we cannot guarantee that a site's future contents will continue to meet our high standards of quality and educational value. Be advised that students should be closely supervised whenever they access the Internet.

Index